CHAPTER 1

INTRODUCTION

The wrong picture is not worth a thousand words. No photo, no electronic impulse can substitute for direct on-the scene knowledge of the key factors in a given country or region. No matter how spectacular a photo may be it cannot reveal enough about plans, intentions, internal political dynamics, economics, etc. There are simply too many cases where photos are ambiguous or useless, and electronic intelligence can drown the analyst in partial or conflicting information. Technical collection is of little help in the most difficult problem of all–political intentions. This is where clandestine human intelligence can make a difference.
— Mark W. Pearce, "The Evolution of Defense
HUMINT through Post Conflict Iraq"

Background

According to Joint Publication 2.0, intelligence is: "the product resulting from the collection, processing, integration, evaluation, analysis, and interpretation of available information concerning foreign nations, hostile or potentially hostile forces or elements, or areas of actual or potential operations."[1]

Joint intelligence is what is produced by elements or agencies of more than one service of the same nation, such as an Army, Navy, or Federal Defense agency. Intelligence results from collecting, processing, analyzing, evaluating, and integrating. It is far more than just collection of information about a threat or area. Intelligence shapes a commander's decision process, and attempts to make predictive assumptions of value to a commander. Again, Joint Publication 2.0 states that "information is of greatest value when it contributes to the commander's decision-making process by providing reasoned

---

[1] Joint Chiefs of Staff, Joint Publication (JP) 2-0, *Intelligence* (Washington, DC: The Joint Staff, 2013), GL-8.

insight into future conditions or situations."[2] Intelligence is conducted at several levels, but in dealing with levels of war or conflict, there are three levels: strategic, operational, and tactical. Strategic intelligence is concerned with the national intelligence produced for the President, the National Defense Security Council, Congress, and other, and supports operations that could affect national security of the country or its allies. The operational intelligence level is mainly used by commanders at the combatant command level, or those that are below the strategic level. Tactical intelligence is used by commanders and planners that are conducting battles and engagements and specific missions.

Human Intelligence

Human Intelligence (HUMINT) is an intelligence collection methodology that deals with the gathering of information and intelligence from human sources through screening, liaison, debriefing, interrogations, and military source operations.[3] HUMINT collection generally requires more time and resources to gather assets and analyze information, oftentimes making it more difficult to produce and implement. "Even though it may seem costly, HUMINT is far less expensive than the various technical collectors, although it still involves costs for training, special equipment, and the accoutrements clandestine officers need to build successful cover stories."[4] The

---

[2] Ibid., I-1.

[3] Headquarters, Department of the Army, Army Doctrinal Reference Publication 2-0, *Intelligence* (Washington, DC: Government Printing Office, August 2012).

[4] Mark M. Lowenthal, *Intelligence: From Secrets to Policy*, 5th ed. (Washington, DC: CQ Press, 2012), 107.

discipline of HUMINT is the oldest methodology for collecting information and intelligence, and has been used in virtually every major conflict throughout history. A HUMINT collector can accomplish his or her mission objectives with little additional logistical assistance needed than that of regular, conventional ground forces, and is not restricted by technology. Their expertise and insights can provide insight not otherwise obtained through other capabilities. "Clandestine sources may make up only 10 or 20 percent of the inputs to intelligence analysis, but agent reports can provide insights that are truly valuable."[5] Even before the advent of technological advances, such as photography or radio communications, intelligence was gathered by the observation from human collectors who had specific placement and access to information through sources, and then reports were given to convey this information. Further, by assimilating or blending in with a group, a collector could gather even more detailed information by being at or near the source, and where that was not possible, by enlisting another human collector that could. The espionage trade was developed by using the technology available at the time, and incorporating any means available to collect relevant intelligence.

The Role of HUMINT

With shrinking budgets, reduction in manning, and an eye for procuring greater technology and equipment, the importance of maintaining a robust HUMINT discipline is essential. Although un-manned intelligence collection has produced faster, larger-scoped,

---

[5] Arthur S. Hulnick, *Fixing the Spy Machine Preparing American Intelligence for the Twenty-First Century* (Westport, CT: Praeger, 1999), 36.

and increased sizes of databases in a relatively short time frame, it still does not provide the context or the predictive measure of human behavior that a person on the ground can.

At the completion of virtually every major conflict, the HUMINT discipline appears to suffer drawdowns and reductions disproportionate to other collection disciplines. Whether it is the dazzle of new technology or the promise of more concrete results, the losses to experienced HUMINT collection teams goes beyond just an asset. The loss is to a complete capability that provides insight and context into future actions, rather than simply showing what is happening now. HUMINT is arguably the only capability that deals with potential future actions and situations, and can interpret subtleties far beyond simply providing an image or recording. When eliminating or reducing this capability, we eliminate proven, trained individuals that cannot be created overnight.

Human Intelligence has been at the forefront for why the United States invaded Iraq in 2003, with the intelligence provided by the source Curveball, which will be discussed in chapter 2. HUMINT was also the intelligence discipline that triggered the chain of collection efforts that ultimately led to the elimination of Osama bin Laden. Starting from interrogations made in the detention center located at Guantanamo, Cuba, then triggering clandestine source operations, and ultimately cueing technology based collection efforts that produced detailed aerial imagery of Bin Laden's compound that gave President Obama a clear picture of Bin Laden's location and security situation.

As technology advances, so do the ways in which we collect intelligence. However, when we rely on one aspect of technology over another, or, over all others, we greatly reduce our clarity on the specifics of the intelligence we collect. Simply gathering a large number of high resolution imagery pictures, or lengthy radio-tele communications alone will not show the intent of the adversary we are collecting information on. By incorporating a HUMINT collection team or analysis element, we can add more detailed context to those communications or imagery pictures, and give a more complete assessment of the situation for a commander or decision maker. Likewise, a HUMINT source operation may lead to the use of an Unmanned Aerial Vehicle (UAV) to gain clarity on unclear details provided by a source, and give specifics to a sources information. Technology can give us an insight into what is happening in the present, but without the human factor, we lose the predictive aspect. This incorporation of multiple collection disciplines is referred to as cross-cueing, and can reduce confusion or contradicting information.

A Changing Threat

In an ever changing environment where our adversaries are not clearly identifiable by uniforms, formations, or even by borders, it is becoming increasingly difficult to pinpoint who is an adversary, let alone their intentions. The threat faced today has changed from what we faced in previous conflicts. As the environment changes, the threats we face adapts and change with it. With threat groups that claim no borders, no nation state affiliation, and no large-scale military formations, it is nearly impossible to determine who or how many members are even associated with a threat group. The Director of National Intelligence James R. Clapper states that "In my 50 years of intelligence experience, the country has never confronted a more diverse array of threats, crises and challenges around the world."[6] The threat environment is changing, and the way we conduct intelligence collection needs to change as well. The hybrid threat presents a new challenge in how we conduct intelligence collection, but also presents an opportunity to fuse and streamline our collection capabilities. "As the hybrid threat increases and resources become more constrained, paired with competing needs for various intelligence assets, the need for talented HUMINT collectors is more essential now than ever."[7]

Opportunities and Challenges with UAV Technology

As technology advanced, so did our dependence on it, but we have also been able to take advantage of opportunities that technology provided. We rely on UAVs as the dominant form of intelligence collection in today's military operations. UAVs can give real-time information on what is happening on the ground, and allow a commander to make quick decisions that will often times save lives. Improvised Explosive Devices have been thwarted by having UAVs detect signatures that identify their location, as well as by actually observing their emplacement. This has resulted in lives being saved directly by this technology, and it has proven its value to the commander. UAVs have also been able to show real-time movement of threat groups, large scale formations, or groups gathering for protests—meetings, as well as give commanders an aerial view of what's happening

---

[6] Claudette Roulo, "Cuts Make Intelligence Failures Likely, Top Intel Official Says," *American Forces Press Service*, April 2013, accessed May 15, 2014, http://www.defense.gov/news/newsarticle.aspx?id=119809.

[7] Colonel Kevin R. Wilkinson, United States Army, "Unparalleled Need: Human Intelligence Collectors in the United States Army" (Strategy Research Project, U.S. Army War College, Carlisle Barracks, PA, 2013), 21.

during an operation as it unfolds. "UAVs can get closer to a target without being detected and does not risk the life of a pilot, because they are operated remotely from miles away."[8] We have come to rely on this technology because it gives us immediate feedback, and there are no reports to read in order to be informed, you can simply watch the video feed, even at your desk. All this with no direct risk to the life of the collector, has made the UAV, and all un-manned collection platforms, the go-to discipline when referring to Intelligence, Surveillance, and Reconnaissance (ISR).

However, this technology also presents several challenges to intelligence collection. After years of conflict in different operational environments, governments and militaries have embraced technological advances that speed up the process of information and intelligence collection. Increasing use of un-manned vehicles and collection assets has been embraced as the direction for the future of intelligence collection. "This nexus of intelligence and technology is like a new toy for a small child. The President, the CIA, and the entire intelligence community have become infatuated with the capabilities of these constantly evolving tools of war."[9] By taking the "human factor" out of the equation, it reduces risk and potential loss of life of the collector, and greatly decreases external costs associated with human-based aspects, such as medical treatment, benefits, and even hesitation. Commanders at most levels, from tactical to strategic, as well as our nation's top civilian leaders, refer to ISR with a meaning of aerial manned and unmanned vehicles; "ISR systems include reconnaissance satellites, some of which have been

---

[8] Lowenthal, *Intelligence: From Secrets to Policy*, 92.

[9] Gabriel Margolis, "The Lack of HUMINT: A Recurring Intelligence Problem," *Global Security Studies* 4, no. 2 (Spring 2013): 54.

operational for decades; Unmanned Aerial Systems of various sizes; and manned aircraft and other sensor platforms"[10] and with exceptions inside the Special Operations community, seldom include ground or human collection capabilities in the realm of ISR. However, as President Obama points out, "it is not possible for America to simply deploy a team of Special Forces to capture every terrorist."[11]

Intelligence, Surveillance, and Reconnaissance is not simply one platform used to conduct intelligence gathering, but rather it is "an activity that synchronizes and integrates the planning and operation of sensors, assets, and processing, exploitation, and dissemination systems in direct support of current and future operations."[12] No one system or capability alone is the basis for ISR, and likewise, no one capability should be perceived by anyone as the best way to collect intelligence. "The U.S. intelligence culture tends to focus on technical means of intelligence like GEOINT, SIGINT, and MASINT."[13] Different situations call for different capabilities, but all collectively make up ISR, including analysis and dissemination.

---

[10] Marshall Curtis Erwin, *Intelligence, Surveillance, and Reconnaissance (ISR) Acquisition: Issues for Congress* (Washington, DC: Congressional Research Service, April 2013), 1.

[11] Guy Taylor and Kristina Wong, "Drone Strikes Plummet as U.S. Seeks more Human Intelligence," *The Washington Times*, October 9, 2013, accessed September 23, 2014, http://www.washingtontimes.com/news/2013/oct/9/drone-strikes-drop-as-us-craves-more-human-intelli/?page=all.

[12] Headquarters, Department of the Army, Army Doctrinal Reference Publication 2-0, *Intelligence*, 1-1.

[13] Richard J. Aldrich and John Kasuku, *Escaping from American Intelligence: Culture, Ethnocentrism and the Anglosphere* 88, no. 5 (September 2012): 50.

During World War II, the collection of intelligence on an industrial scale was through radio monitoring and code-breaking, taking advantage of the technology of the time. "However, it seems that when operations are conducted based solely upon technical intelligence, incorrect human intelligence, or without human intelligence at all, some of the greatest failures in CIA history have occurred."[14]

In more than a decade of conflict, intelligence collection has seen rapid changes and improvements, both domestically and in theaters of operation. We can watch UAV real-time feeds of Coalition operations from our personal work stations. We can see areas virtually unreachable by man as clear as if we were standing there. We can push our intelligence collection further, faster, and higher, all the while nearly eliminating the risk of human casualties with intelligence collectors and those who support them.

Assumptions and Limitations

The first assumption is that intelligence capabilities will be decreased across the board in line with reductions in personnel, and no specific collection discipline will be eliminated. Personnel reductions will have the same effects on intelligence collection disciplines overall, and will therefore not adversely affect HUMINT any more or less than other collection methods. With fewer collectors, there is the likelihood that we will get fewer intelligence reports, but this is the same for HUMINT as well as technology-based collection methods.

---

[14] Margolis, "The Lack of HUMINT: A Recurring Intelligence Problem," 44.

The second assumption is that technology will get better, faster, and even smaller almost exponentially. As technology advances, it will be continually integrated with methods of intelligence collection.

The third assumption is that HUMINT is not fully integrated with technical means of intelligence collection, and looked at as a collection discipline that cannot provide the same immediate feedback of information that commanders and decision makers want today. With technological advances that provide real-time, immediate feedback with decreased risk to human life, HUMINT is not seen as an equally relevant collection methodology.

The last assumption is that intelligence failures are the result of not fully integrated intelligence across collection, interpretation, analysis, and dissemination. Intelligence sharing does happen, but not at the level desired, which leads to claims of intelligence failures.

There are several limitations in this paper, the first of which is that secondary sources were used in research. No direct interviews with commanders or decision makers were conducted. Further, commander's views on HUMINT and intelligence collection were mostly pulled from negative reviews of intelligence collection, which creates a reporting bias. Another limitation is the personal bias form which this paper has been written, in that I come from a HUMINT background, and have experience in HUMINT collection in Operation Iraqi Freedom. Finally, the time available for research was limiting the number of reports and views on HUMINT collection and reporting.

CHAPTER 2

LITERATURE REVIEW

The hypothesis for this research paper is that intelligence collection can be enhanced by integrating HUMINT collection with technology-based collection methods, specifically UAVs, and making intelligence sharing and dissemination more user-friendly. With reductions in both personnel and budgets, combined with an increasingly changing threat environment, it is important to study how intelligence collection can keep pace with these constraints. The Hybrid Threat has become more sophisticated, and poses a greater challenge to intelligence collection. Relying on individual collection disciplines alone cannot give the level of detail commanders and decision makers need. With fewer personnel and shrinking budgets, HUMINT and technology-based collection methods must compliment each other, and the results must be disseminated timely and widely.

This paper will examine works across four main focus areas: Decreasing the HUMINT capability, HUMINT capabilities in conjunction with technical capabilities, specifically UAVs, HUMINT successes and failures, and HUMINT reporting and dissemination issues.

Focus Area: Decreasing the HUMINT Capability

When examining an abstract concept of relevancy or necessity, we can look at how intelligence collection is organized, specifically, after conflicts, and how collection assets are arranged, built up or reduced. Generally, intelligence capabilities are built-up, across all disciplines, during times of conflict. Commanders and decision makers need real-time, relevant information in order to make decisions. The more they have, the better

11

informed they are, and can make timely decisions that best capitalize on the intelligence about terrain, enemy, environment. However, at the completion of major conflicts and wars, budgetary restrictions dictate that downsizing is necessary. Downsizing in intelligence is no different than other branches, and ultimately collection will suffer.

Director of National Intelligence, Clapper cites that the past decade has been a rebuilding time for intelligence, but, "Sequestration forces the intelligence community to reduce all intelligence activities and functions without regard to impact on our mission . . . the cuts jeopardize the nation's safety and security, and that the jeopardy will increase over time."[15] In Roulo's work, Clapper's perspective on this is from the idea that by decreasing intelligence without regard to mission, our nation will be less safe. His views come after a decade of conflict with a changing threat, and after direct attacks against United States. His view does not take into consideration the possibility of having no loss to intelligence collection simply because of reductions, and this paper will seek to address the idea of intelligence collection continuing to provide valuable information to commanders while operating under reduction constraints.

Looking back, historically we have reduced our capabilities after times of conflicts and wars, as the threat is not seen as imminent anymore. After the "peace dividend," a political slogan used to describe the economic benefit of a decrease in defense spending, put forth by President George H.W. Bush in the early 1990s, intelligence collection has been reduced, to include HUMINT collectors, with an estimated 23 percent in total reductions.[16] The reductions to HUMINT were in line with

---

[15] Roulo, "Cuts Make Intelligence Failures Likely, Top Intel Official Says."

[16] Ibid.

reductions to other collection disciplines, and the President's perspective was operating

under a decreased need of intelligence collection under this new peace dividend, as well

as budget restraints. Taken at face value, the information simply states total reductions

were 23 percent, and does not indicate any loss in capability, either to HUMINT or to

other collections methods. Loss of manpower can be felt more widely than loss of

equipment alone, as personnel are required for the analysis of the collected information.

Furthermore, well trained personnel, with specific expertise, such as language ability,

cannot be acquired as easily as can commercial technology.

Of course losing personnel can affect any intelligence collection discipline, but

the HUMINT disciplines were the most affected by drawdowns. "This loss of manpower

was devastating, particularly in our two most manpower intensive activities: all-source

analysis and human source collection."[17] Steven Leary's work was done in a time under

budget cuts while the United States was conducting operations in two theaters, Iraq and

Afghanistan. With two major operations, as well as smaller operations world wide,

reductions were felt heavily. The perspective was that by reducing manpower in areas

that were HUMINT intensive, we would reduce the ability to collect intelligence. Leary's

perspective does not, however, consider the capabilities of technical collection, and how

they could enhance HUMINT collection. This research paper attempts to find a way

where technical collection and HUMINT collection can enhance overall intelligence

production, while operating under constraints of reduction and finances. When we reduce

personnel, we reduce collection assets and analysis capability. The hard truth is that

---

[17] Stephen Leary, "Intelligence Budgets During the Clinton Years," September 2008, accessed May 13, 2014, http://blog.stephenleary.com/2008/09/intelligence-budgets-during-clinton.html.

technological equipment does not count against end-strength numbers for a budget conscious military in a downsizing period. If we look at downsizing our end strength numbers, it obviously comes out of people, and thus the HUMINT discipline will lose people as the rest of the disciplines will. However, this loss is not only in personnel, but in knowledge and training; they are the collection capability.

Looking back to pre-era Bush and Clinton, the intelligence cuts were also felt heavily in the 1970s, especially with reductions to HUMINT collection. By the end of the decade, "Jimmy Carter's Director of Central Intelligence, Admiral Stansfield Turner, by opting for technology-heavy collection methods, cemented the congressional hit-job by emasculating the CIA's most valuable & effective resource—its Human Intelligence (HUMINT) assets."[18] Again, we see a perspective where the reductions to HUMINT are seen as catastrophic. The view of the author is clearly slanted towards how the Central Intelligence Agency conducts its operations, which are primarily through HUMINT collection. It does not, however, address how these favored technology-heavy collection methods can enhance the loss of HUMINT collectors and analysis, as this paper attempts to do. The post September 11th time period is no different, "In nearly every respect, these events [9/11] demonstrated what America's intelligence services lacked most: an effective HUMINT capability, sufficient foreign language capacity, infiltration (or even a basic understanding) of the global Islamist terrorist network, and experience with effective post-conflict reconstruction and insurgency tactics."[19] Understanding that this

---

[18] John C. Wobensmith and Jeff Smith, "Reinvigorating Intelligence," *The Journal of International Security Affairs* (Spring 2007), accessed May 15, 2014, http://www.securityaffairs.org/issues/2007/12/wobensmith&smith.php.

[19] Ibid.

perspective is that after the attacks conducted on September 11th, 2001, if we reduce our intelligence collection, specifically HUMINT, we will fail in identifying and addressing emerging threats. These views do not incorporate other means of intelligence collection, such as technological means, which this paper will address in chapters 4 and 5.

The implication is that by cutting our HUMINT collection capability, we will somehow suffer a proportionate loss in collection of information. If the sole source of intelligence collection is HUMINT, then you can see where this would affect an organizations ability to collect. However, with a reduced immediate need, such as an ongoing or developing conflict or war, is it responsible to maintain a capability just in case, where there may be an opportunity to augment or enhance a capability through other collection methods or through sharing and dissemination.

Obviously by cutting any capability, you run the risk of reducing the output. This however, does not indicate that it is no longer relevant. HUMINT is the collection discipline that comes off as the simplest to reduce, as it encompasses mainly personnel. There are other more costly collection disciplines that could be reduced to save money, while not sacrificing overall collection. "HUMINT is one of the most inexpensive and effective means of intelligence collection."[20] When researchers such as Colonel Kevin R. Wilkinson claim that HUMINT is the most inexpensive means of collection, it appears as though they refer to the immediate collection capability, and do not consider the other factors of upkeep that would also be present in technology based collection systems. The cost of utilizing a HUMINT collector's source for a meeting, for example, is relatively

---

[20] Wilkinson, "Unparalleled Need: Human Intelligence Collectors in the United States Army," 7.

15

inexpensive when compared to the launch, mission, and asset recovery costs for an unmanned UAV flight. However, "Overall budget requirements for HUMINT are dwarfed by the major investment required for satellites and signals intelligence collection."[21] The perspective is that HUMINT is overall less expensive. However, what this perspective lacks, are the factors of support that HUMINT requires, such as logistics support, life support, and technical dissemination requirements.

Wilkinson states that "Regardless of technological advances and the transcending threat environment, HUMINT remains the most reliable and economical collection asset to determine a nation's objectives and motivations."[22] However, what he omits is what's important in today's Hybrid Threat; the fact that we are largely not dealing with nations, but with factions not tied to any state, so when he asserts that it is the most reliable collection asset to determine a nation's objectives, we cannot assume it will be the same for non-state actors or groups with no nation affiliation. His perspective is limited to previous methods of war and engagements.

Perhaps one reason why a specific intelligence collection capability is seen as more productive or relevant, is in the level that it is user-friendly, or easily accessible. As stated, UAV feeds can be seen by many, with the proper classification and access, at their own workstations. Results are immediate and relatively understandable in that they show images of recognizable features and terrain. We can actually see groups of people, groups of vehicles, houses and structures. A real time image is displayed of what's happening at

---

[21] Richard A. Best, Jr., *Intelligence to Counter Terrorism: Issues for Congress* (Washington, DC: Congressional Research Service, May 2003), 9.

[22] Wilkinson, "Unparalleled Need: Human Intelligence Collectors in the United States Army," 9.

the selected location. HUMINT does not provide that real time, user-friendly result that top leaders and commanders want. "The general lack of understanding about what HUMINT actually does, and the results it produces, greatly impacts its use as a viable collection capability. When all levels of leadership fail to understand the roles, responsibilities, and requirements for a HUMINT collector, the capability is often underutilized, and seen as excess personnel."[23] Wilkinson's perspective may be biased, as there is no alternative aspect presented of how commanders have successfully used and integrated HUMINT collection. If a capability is seen as excess, or not producing results, whether fully understood or not, it becomes an obvious choice for reduction, thus decreasing its relevancy, or at least its potential for relevancy.

During both Operation Iraqi Freedom and Operation Enduring Freedom, there was a surge in troop strength across the board, in all occupational specialties, including Military Intelligence. The focus, it seemed, was at the tactical level, or the Brigade Combat Teams. Top leaders saw the need and importance for a robust intelligence collection effort, particularly with the new Hybrid Threat.

Retired Lieutenant General John Frederick "Jeff" Kimmons was a strong supporter of not only robust intelligence collection during both operations in Iraq and Afghanistan, but also a strong advocate for bolstering the military's HUMINT collection capability. In 2006, he told the annual Association of the U.S. Army convention in Washington that "the service is increasing the number of military intelligence personnel at the brigade and battalion levels and expanding its human intelligence HUMINT

---

[23] Ibid., 19.

capabilities."[24] However, these statements were made during times of troop surges, and offer different perspectives than those made during times of troop reductions after conflicts.

Lieutenant General Kimmons goes on to state that the Army also plans on building four new interrogation battalions with 84 interrogators in each, and creating HUMINT plans and operations cells in each of its divisions and brigade combat teams, as well as establishing a HUMINT joint training center of excellence at the Army's Intelligence Center and School at Fort Huachuca, Arizona.[25]

Lieutenant General Kimmons saw the need to change the way intelligence is collected when facing an asymmetric threat, or, a Hybrid Threat. Making intelligence dissemination flat, so that it could be easily shared with those needing the information to make decisions, was one of his goals for integrating intelligence reporting. "To accomplish these tasks, the Army is forming from 8 to 10 Military Intelligence collection battalions heavily weighted with HUMINT source-handler and interrogator capabilities."[26] Again, this perspective is from an Army leader during the time of troop surges during two operations in two separate theaters.

However, during two simultaneous operations in two different theaters, while facing an asymmetric, hybrid threat, intelligence build-up only made sense. Kimmons further states, "More than 90 percent of that growth (by 2013) will be aligned with

---

[24] Lt. Gen. John F. Kimmons, "Intel Surge," *Aviation Week and Space Technology* 165, no. 19 (November 13, 2006), 1.

[25] Ibid.

[26] Ibid.

enhanced tactical collection and analysis. Army HUMINT capacity will increase more than any other intelligence discipline and will more than double in strength."[27] Lieutenant General Kimmon's perspective addresses the new Hybrid Threat, and military collection capabilities, specifically HUMINT capabilities, would benefit the fight against this new threat, but not just in collection alone, also through integration and dissemination. Collection of intelligence is only half the picture. If this collected information, when properly analyzed and evaluated, is not disseminated into the hands that need it to make decisions, then it is essentially just fodder for databases.

Major General Robert P. Ashley, Commanding General of the Army's Intelligence Center of Excellence and Fort Huachuca, Arizona, also sees the need to restructure how the Army conducts intelligence collection. In October of 2014 he highlighted changes to intelligence collection through a new Battlefield Surveillance Brigade being redesignated as an expeditionary military intelligence brigade. Although this new brigade is smaller than previous ones, "The unit would be adaptable, able to deploy as part of the Global Response Force, or in support of any number of operations across the globe."[28] He goes on to state that "The Army eventually will have three expeditionary military intelligence brigades . . . they are being created based on lessons learned from the past several years, and will help provide information commanders can

---

[27] Ibid., 2.

[28] Drew Brooks, "525th Military Intelligence Brigade unveiled on Fort Bragg," *Fayetteville Observer*, October 2014, accessed October 17, 2014, http://www.fayobserver.com/news/local/th-military-intelligence-brigade-unveiled-on-fort-bragg/article_fa19cc96-f895-59f3-accb-eb9015281b15.html?mode=jqm.

use to prevent wars and, if needed, to fight and win."[29] He noted that the transformation of the Battlefield Surveillance Brigade "marked the latest step toward the future for Army intelligence, which is adapting to the challenge of a complex world."[30] Ashley's perspective indeed looks toward the future of intelligence collection against a new, Hybrid Threat.

Focus Area: Man and Machine the HUMINT Capability and the UAV

UAVs and other aerial platforms have become the latest feather in the cap of intelligence collection. Referred to as:

> One of the most significant military developments in the last 10 to 15 years has been that of the unmanned aerial vehicle, which has evolved from the simple drone with limited capability to today's sophisticated aircraft, which, for some roles, particularly Intelligence, Surveillance and Reconnaissance, is now the platform of choice.[31]

The perspective of UAVs is that they provide a previously unattainable aerial view of situations on the ground to aid commanders in the decision making process. They have advanced intelligence collection with technology that reduces risk to the collectors.

UAVs have the ability to stay over a target area for longer periods of time, undetected, with no risk to human life. This advantage does indeed make them an invaluable and relevant collection asset.

---

[29] Ibid.

[30] Ibid.

[31] Hugh Jameson, "Drones between Satellite and Earth," *Armada International* 31, no. 6 (December 2007/January 2008): 54.

Citizens in the United States today have become almost numb to the fact that they are under constant surveillance. In malls, shopping centers, schools, sporting events, the ATM, and almost anywhere public business takes places, cameras record our activities. While this is not by definition "intelligence collection," it shows the ease in which surveillance can be done, with a commercial camera purchased virtually anywhere, and a basic user manual. If a wire is cut or a battery no longer good, it can be easily replaced. There is no specific skill set inherent in the equipment, that is to say, it is ready to perform as advertised upon the flip of a switch or button.

HUMINT without UAV Technology

Human Intelligence is the collection discipline that comes off as the simplest to reduce, as it encompasses mainly personnel. It has been said by many HUMINT collectors that what the HUMINT professional lacks with technology, they make up for with training and innate skills, skills and training that cannot be purchased, but must be invested in. However, this is a skill set that needs to be continually practiced and exercised to remain sharp. "Even in today's era of irregular warfare, the fine art of collecting human source intelligence has in large part become lost thanks to the relative comfort afforded by partner relationships and advances in intelligence technology."[32] We are relying on technology to do the finesse work of establishing relationships with people that can have the potential to reveal future intentions.

However, in 2013, the need to at least begin adding a human element in conjunction with drones and UAVs was addressed. "The number of drone strikes

---

[32] Robert D. Steele, "Human Intelligence: All Humans, All Minds, All the Time" (Monograph, Strategic Studies Institute, U.S. Army War College, May 2010), 21.

approved by the Obama Administration on suspected terrorists has fallen dramatically

this year, [2013] as the war with al Qaeda increasingly shifts to Africa and U.S.

intelligence craves more captures and interrogations of high-value targets."[33] The value is

seen in that by capturing and interrogating these high-value targets, information can be

obtained and provide intelligence about a network or organization that technical

collection methods alone cannot produce.

HUMINT with UAV Technology

We can gather imagery and details otherwise impossible to get, and even strike

targets while maintaining constant surveillance. UAVs can conduct very specific,

targeted strikes; "Targeted, or personality strikes utilize all forms of intelligence

available, including HUMINT. Targeted strikes utilize HUMINT because they are used

to target top tier leadership of terrorist organizations; a specific person."[34] Working

together, HUMINT can provide specificity for targeting that utilizes UAV systems, or

future times and locations on where a target may plan to be. "Today's enemy is

embedded in local populations. Drones have no way of distinguishing between enemy

combatants and noncombatants without actionable intelligence. Deep knowledge of

today's enemies is vital to understanding them, and defeating them."[35]

---

[33] Taylor, and Wong, "Drone Strikes Plummet as U.S. Seeks more Human Intelligence."

[34] Margolis, "The Lack of HUMINT: A Recurring Intelligence Problem," 55.

[35] Robert Caruso, "Here's How the US Can Build the Intelligence Capabilities Needed to Defeat ISIS," *Business Insider*, September 2014, accessed September 23, 2014, http://www.businessinsider.co.id/the-us-needs-better-humint-to-beat-isis-2014-9/#.VEWDybQo6P8.

Without the human factor, we would be far less likely to predict the where or when a target may present itself, and merely rely on luck, or right place, right time circumstances. It is the fusion of technology with human insight that will ultimately produce the best picture with the most detailed analysis. Technology does not operate without human interaction, and, likewise, human analysis and reporting is enhanced with technology. Ultimately, "by restoring human primacy in relation to all technical intelligence operations, technical intelligence will excel with HUMINT, not alone."[36] "When U.S. soldiers are on the ground for a raid . . . it means they can 'collect additional materials of intelligence value from the dwelling, further assisting in the planning of follow-on operations.'"[37] This is just one example for using a combination of collection disciplines to enhance the situational awareness for a commander or decision maker who is not physically there. It is these collaborations that, when combined, deepen our understanding of a threat and the environment they operate in.

Focus Area: HUMINT Successes and Failures

There are many examples of where HUMINT can be seen as both success and failure throughout past and present conflicts. No one can say with certainty that if HUMINT were better utilized, that the outcome would have been different. But, looking at some of the areas where HUMINT was capitalized on, we can see its direct influence. However, it becomes clear that when HUMINT and technology are combined, or support each other, collection, fidelity and detail are increased, as is situational understanding.

---

[36] Steele, "Human Intelligence: All Humans, All Minds, All the Time," 10.

[37] Taylor and Wong, "Drone Strikes Plummet as U.S. Seeks more Human Intelligence."

After the Bay of Pigs, the US intelligence community was challenged by the Cuban Missile Crisis. The Cuban Missile Crisis occurred between the United States and the Soviet Union during October 1965, over the placement of Soviet missiles in Cuba. Manned U-2 reconnaissance flights over Cuba discovered the movement of missiles utilizing imaging. The CIA "had discovered the missiles, which it deemed capable of striking the United States, on 14 of October 1962, and corroborating intelligence was received from a Cuban refugee on 20 September 1962 that he had seen a Russian missile on a truck in Cuba."[38]

However, the United States had a HUMINT source, Oleg Penkovsky, a Colonel in Soviet military intelligence that provided invaluable intelligence to the United States beginning in 1961.[39] "Penkovsky's debriefing sessions produced about 1,200 pages of transcripts, which CIA and MI-6 had around 30 translators and analysts working on. The Colonel's information was immensely valuable, helping dispel concerns about Soviet strategic superiority, and showing that the United States had the advantage in missile systems."[40] The intelligence that Penkovsky provided showed the time the Soviet missiles took to assemble and become functional, which allowed President Kennedy time to work on diplomacy. The perspective is that without the HUMINT source and

---

[38] Michael A. Turner, *Historical Dictionary of United States Intelligence* (Lanham, MD: Scarecrow Press, 2005), 46.

[39] Margolis, "The Lack of HUMINT: A Recurring Intelligence Problem," 52.

[40] Central Intelligence Agency, "The Capture and Execution of Colonel Penkovsky, 1963," accessed September 23, 2014, https://www.cia.gov/news-information/featured-story-archive/2010-featured-story-archive/colonel-penkovsky.html.

intelligence, the administration would have had to rely on imagery alone, and not have the insight into the timeline provided by Penkovsky that proved invaluable.

However one defines success or failure, it is largely accepted that when a tragic event or attack occurs, and the Intelligence Community did not know about it ahead of time, it is seen as a failure of intelligence. The question is always asked, "how did we not see this coming?"

> Infiltrating a terror clique to obtain detailed planning information, the truly accurate information—is extremely difficult. We do information technology without peer, but in the dirty, gray world of James Bond cloak-and-dagger deception, we're Joe Average. America's gravest intelligence weakness is a lack of HUMINT, human spies, capable of penetrating al Qaeda.[41]

Austin Bay's post 9/11 article takes a look at how Defense Secretary Donald Rumsfeld viewed intelligence collection in the wake of the biggest terrorist attack on American soil, and how the Intelligence Community has failed. With this new hybrid threat, the technological advances alone were not going to produce the intelligence needed to stop, or even predict future attacks. Further, "during the investigation into the events that surrounded the Al Qaida terrorist attacks of 11September, 2001, the 9/11 Commission found that the biggest impediment to all-source analysis is 'the human or systemic resistance to sharing information.'"[42]

Recently, with an increasing threat from the Islamic State of Iraq and Syria, HUMINT collection, or the lack of, is still blamed as an intelligence failure.

---

[41] Austin Bay, "In the Absence of HUMINT," *The Washington Times*, July 31, 2003, accessed May 13, 2014, http://www.washingtontimes.com/news/2003/jul/31/20030731-081957-6447r/?page=all.

[42] Darin Swan, "HUMINT Challenges in the Post 9/11 Era," August 2008, accessed October 13, 2014, http://www.academia.edu/1460547/HUMINT_Challenges_in_the_Post-9_11_Era.

Clandestine human intelligence makes up a surprisingly small percentage of the US intelligence collection effort worldwide. I can say from experience that the U.S. could devote significantly more resources to human-derived information. This lack of HUMINT might have something to do with the lack of warning about ISIS's summer blitz through Iraq and Syria.[43]

Robert Caruso's perspective is that a human failure is at the root for the lack of warning prior to the Islamic State of Iraq and Syria's actions in Iraq and Syria. The implications are that technology based collections methods were sufficient, and the HUMINT arena was lacking. This study does not clarify or stipulate whether or not the technology based collection was indeed satisfactory or conclusive on its own. It is the contention of this paper that without the combination of the human element with technology, and not the lack of HUMINT alone, is the real failure.

In the few years prior to the start of Operation Iraqi Freedom, when the prospect of Weapons of Mass Destruction was thought to be at the forefront of Iraqi President Saddam Hussein's arsenal, HUMINT collection was minimal at best, and almost none of it focused on nuclear, biological or chemical weapons. In the United States Senate's Select Committee on Intelligence's *Report on the US Intelligence Community's Pre War Intelligence Assessments on Iraq* conclusions section, several conclusions were made that indicated a failed use of the HUMINT capability, as well as intelligence collection as a whole. The 2004 report conclusions highlights include specific mention of the single human source CURVEBALL. "The committee also found that Defense HUMINT Services demonstrated serious lapses in its handling of the human source code named

---

[43] Caruso, "Here's How the US Can Build the Intelligence Capabilities Needed to Defeat ISIS."

CURVEBALL, who was the principle source behind the Intelligence Community's assessment that Iraq had a mobile, biological weapons program."[44]

But perhaps the final straw in how the Intelligence Community fails to share information and reporting is seen again in the Senate Select Committee's report, in the final paragraph of conclusion six, where they state "The process by which the Intelligence Community . . . shares sensitive human intelligence is skewed too heavily toward withholding information . . . particularly after the lack of information sharing was found to have played a key role in the intelligence failures of 9/11."[45]

What is not clear when referring to intelligence failures is, what specifically failed. Placing blame on not collecting enough intelligence about a specific threat or region, to how the information is shared are not definitive answers as to the question of why intelligence failed, but only point to a breakdown somewhere in the process. One unique perspective on this failure is that "Most failures of battlefield intelligence are due not to insufficient data or intelligence-collection efforts but instead to intelligence products that were either ignored or analytically weak."[46] This suggests that failures may not be the result of collection, by any discipline, or even by the reporting process or dissemination, but rather, by simply not using the products or reports.

---

[44] United States Senate Select Committee on Intelligence, *Report on the US Intelligence Community's Pre War Intelligence Assessments on Iraq*, July 2004.

[45] Ibid.

[46] Lieutenant General William G. Boykin, U.S. Army (ret.) and Scott Swanson, "'Operationalizing' Intelligence," *Special Warfare Bulletin* 6 (June 2008), accessed September 22, 2014, http://www.army.mil/professionalWriting/volumes/volume6/june_2008/6_08_1_pf.html.

Focus Area: HUMINT Reporting Issues

According to US Army Field Manual 2-22.3, intelligence reporting is the final and in many cases the most vital phase in HUMINT collection. If the collected information is not reported accurately, in a timely manner, in the proper format, and to the correct recipient, it cannot become part of the all-source intelligence product or tip in time to affect operational decisions. Information that would support targeting must be reported by the fastest means possible. Ultimately, the reporting is what makes or breaks the value of intelligence, and the outcomes or actionability from the intelligence. No matter how clandestine, covert or technically acquired, if the relevant intelligence is not put in the hands that need it most, it is ultimately worthless. Hind sight with intelligence may provide lessons learned, but it is still failure.

Field Manual 2-22.3, chapter 10 lays out the importance of intelligence report writing for HUMINT collectors, and cites seven specific areas that each report should contain; accuracy, brevity, clarity, coherence, completeness, timeliness, and releasability, which refers to how widely the information may be distributed, and at what classification.

There are several types of HUMINT reports; Intelligence Information Reports, SALUTE Reports, Basic Source Data Reports, Contact Reports, Screening Reports, Knowledgeability Briefs, Notice of Intelligence Potential, Interrogation Summaries, Termination Reports, Biographic Reports, and others. Not all of these types of reports are relevant to commanders and decision makers at the tactical level, but all will contribute to the overall intelligence picture. Who needs which reports, where can they be found, and how do we get them to the appropriate level is what's often the most confusing aspect of reporting. HUMINT reporting alone has three basic reporting channels; the operational reporting chain, the technical reporting chain, and the intelligence reporting chain. Again,

Field Manual 2-22.3, chapter 10 states:

> Many elements serve multiple and overlapping functions within the reporting architecture. Each element must be aware of its function within the architecture to ensure that information is disseminated expeditiously to the right place in the right format. This architecture should be established and published prior to implementation in order to avoid confusion.[47]

With so many different types of reports, each containing at least seven aspects,

and each reported through different types of channels, it's no wonder that many

commanders become confused and frustrated about accessing relevant HUMINT reports.

In the beginning of Operation Iraqi Freedom in 2003, "combat leaders did not

understand how to use their intelligence specialists . . . Military Intelligence commanders

were frustrated at the misuse of HUMINT assets by maneuver commanders. They also

believed that combat arms officers did not understand HUMINT capabilities."[48]

Furthermore, when the US Senate's Special Committee on Intelligence made their

conclusions in a 2004 report, they cited in conclusion number six that "the CIA continues

to excessively compartment sensitive HUMINT reporting and fails to share important

information about HUMINT reporting and sources with Intelligence Community analysts

who have a need to know."[49] By not sharing information, or by over classifying

---

[47] Headquarters, Department of the Army, Field Manual (FM) 2-22.3, *Human Intelligence Collector Operations* (Washington, DC: Government Printing Office, August 2006), 10-5.

[48] Thomas E. Ricks, *Fiasco: The American Military Adventure in Iraq, 2003 to 2005* (New York: The Penguin Press, 2006), 160.

[49] United States Senate Select Committee on Intelligence, *Report on the US Intelligence Community's Pre War Intelligence Assessments on Iraq*, July 2004.

information so that only a select few will even be able to access it, we have in essence made that report or information irrelevant.

Even from personal experience as an Intelligence Officer and advisor in Iraq from 2007 to 2008, I had witnessed many HUMINT collection teams performing menial duties that allowed them little to no time to perform actual HUMINT collection tasks, such as develop sources or debrief personnel returning from patrols. This was largely due to commanders at all levels, not knowing or understanding the capability that HUMINT provides, and how it can enhance the intelligence picture as a whole. So, from this specific example, when a HUMINT capability is not utilized in a HUMINT capacity, it will not produce any relevant HUMINT reports, thus feeding the cyclical process of commander and combat arms personnel misunderstanding the capability of HUMINT. It's a domino process that builds to misunderstanding, but it can also be a domino process that clears it up as well. As HUMINT reporting is analyzed and cross referenced with other collection disciplines, a clearer picture of future intentions can be made. This will become critical when trying to analyze intent of a hybrid threat, or an enemy that looks like the population it hides amongst.

CHAPTER 3

RESEARCH METHODOLOGY

For the purpose of this study, I chose a qualitative case study methodology based on secondary source documents. This was a comparative research study that looked at views of HUMINT collection and UAV collection separately, as well as combined. Additionally, I looked at studies that compared intelligence sharing, reporting, and dissemination, with a focus on HUMINT. This was a subjective study that attempted to compare and contrast the HUMINT collection methodology and the UAV collection methodology, as well as intelligence sharing. Based on time constraints and available resources, this was the best methodology for this particular research question.

In this methodology, I concentrated on four focus areas, and how HUMINT relates to, and enhances each area. The factors I looked at were: Decreasing the HUMINT Capability, Man and Machine (UAVs), HUMINT Successes and Failures, and Reporting Issues. In each focus area I attempted to view unbiased studies and reports from the specific perspective of the author or their subject of their study or report.

Factors Examined

Decreasing the HUMINT Capability looked at the effects of reductions to HUMINT personnel both during and after conflicts, and how those reductions may affect intelligence collection and dissemination. Historical reductions after major conflicts were examined, as well as recent personnel reductions, as well as increases in HUMINT personnel. The hypothesis was that by decreasing HUMINT personnel the HUMINT capability as a whole will be decreased.

31

Man and machine examined the roles of HUMINT in conjunction with UAVs, as well as operating independently of them. With the advent of the technological advancements provided by the UAV, I examined how HUMINT collection can work in conjunction with UAVs to produce a more detailed look at the threat and environment. The complimentary aspect of UAVs and human collection and analysis is viewed both positively and negatively.

Human Intelligence success and failures attempted to show how HUMINT collection alone has proven successful in intelligence collection that led to decision making, as well as where it failed. There were more studies highlighting the failures of HUMINT, and the human factor, and I attempted to examine the reasons they were viewed as failures.

The last factor examined was the way in which HUMINT reporting is conducted, and how the information is disseminated to commanders and decision makers. I further examined how commanders and decision makers view the HUMINT discipline, and attempted to understand why it was considered "misunderstood."

This research paper attempts to examine multiple sides and opinions on HUMINT collection and the need to either build up or reduce HUMINT collection in the future. Further, how HUMINT can incorporate with technology-based collection methods was looked at. The collection of intelligence as a whole is necessary for commanders to make informed decisions about the operating environment (ADRP 2.0), but exactly which intelligence collection disciplines are necessary or relevant may be immaterial. The fact that intelligence collection helps shape the view of the overall operating environment, terrain, civil factors, and other pertinent aspects is not the focus of this paper, but rather how can HUMINT enhance and work with technology based collection methods, specifically UAVs, to increase a commander's understanding.

By examining the historical facts and documentation, this thesis attempted to compare and contrast uses of HUMINT collection during periods of drawdown and conflict, as well as commander's views of the HUMINT discipline, and how it can enhance other collection disciplines. An advantage to this methodology is that the information already exists, and correlations can be examined between HUMINT and UAVs, and how both disciplines can compliment each other to enhance intelligence collection at large.

CHAPTER 4

ANALYSIS

"Intelligence can provide a competitive advantage only if its various pieces are matched with operational experience and intuition, reasoning and analytical skills honed for the specific situation."[50] In short, if taken independently, intelligence gathered may only provide a partial view of the threat or terrain. It is the combination of the human element and the technology that provides the clearest picture of a threat, or the threat's operating environment.

When examining the relevance of intelligence collection disciplines, specifically HUMINT, it is hard to justify one collection discipline as more or less relevant over others, based on biases of those involved in collection, or those that are consumers of intelligence products. Clearly, when intelligence collection leads to concise and accurate reporting, and then produces actionable targets to engage, whether through lethal means or non-lethal means, it is seen as relevant, necessary and important.

Despite a changing threat or changing environment, intelligence collection is still intended to give commanders and decision makers a clearer picture of what is currently happening, as well as what is likely to happen in the future. It is easy to say, after a tragic event has occurred, or an individual was not apprehended, that intelligence failed us in that we should have seen it coming. Since we were unable to thwart such an attack, or arrest an individual, the causation is made that our intelligence must have failed us.

---

[50] Boykin and Swanson, "'Operationalizing' Intelligence."

Decreasing the HUMINT Capability

Despite previous assumptions on the downsizing of HUMINT capabilities, no evidence suggests that HUMINT, or any other collection capability is being specifically targeted for downsizing. While budget constraints will affect how intelligence collection may focus its efforts, they are not being targeted to reduce collection or specific HUMINT systems. In fact, there is evidence that suggests that some commanders and leaders see the need for increasing HUMINT's role in intelligence collection, specifically in dealing with a changing threat environment, where our adversaries often blend in with local populations, and claim no affiliation with any nation state. Less reporting is offset by the incorporation of collection disciplines, like HUMINT with imagery intelligence, in order to produce more detailed analysis and a clearer picture of not only what is happening on the ground in the present, but what implications that may have on future actions or intentions.

The articles and essays claiming that a downsizing of HUMINT will likely put us in jeopardy of having more intelligence failures, just do not add up, and come off as facts interpreted to meet specific claims. James Clapper states that cuts in intelligence activities will ultimately jeopardize our nation's safety and security. September 11th, 2001 is often cited as a reason why we need more intelligence collection and that where we lack the most fidelity in collection is in HUMINT. The United States Senate Select Subcommittee on Intelligence stated that the lack of information sharing was key in the intelligence failures of 9/11. The assumption is that because the attack was not prevented, intelligence sharing failed in alerting the right decision makers so that they could have enacted a plan to prevent the attacks. The analysis of this is that there was at least sufficient intelligence available that would have indicated or predicted some type of attack, but it was just not shared or disseminated properly through the right channels or to the right decision makers in a timely manner.

Less intelligence does not mean less safe or more susceptible to attack, as a nation. Likewise, more intelligence does not mean more relevant. The right intelligence disseminated to the right decision makers is what's more relevant.

Reductions in force, whether personnel or equipment, are a constraint that must be operated within, by intelligence professionals as well as combat arms and maneuver professionals, thus leveling the playing field for operating under constraints. Evidence does not suggest that HUMINT is being reduced disproportionally at rates higher than other collection disciplines. HUMINT is getting smaller in line with reductions across the board, whether within the military or other intelligence agencies. The fact that a capability is being reduced does not mean it cannot still be relevant, or produce products and reports that are of value. This reduction on capability must simply be addressed as to how best to utilize the HUMINT capability in conjunction with other capabilities. Top leaders see the advantages of technology with the future of intelligence collection, but also realize the importance of incorporating human input and analysis.

When Major General Ashley, Commanding General of the Army's Intelligence Center of Excellence and Fort Huachuca, Arizona recognizes that the environment intelligence professionals are operating in has changed, he understands that changing to fit that environment is the answer, even if it is with less personnel.

Man and Machine: HUMINT and the UAV

When Gabriel Margolis states that the President of the United States, as well as the entire Intelligence Community have become infatuated with the capabilities of technology, even comparing them to a child with a new toy, he does not say that they have abandoned non technical means of intelligence collection. Clearly though, the Intelligence Community has high regards for, and places considerable focus on technical means of intelligence collection. When it comes down to risk to human life, the technical collection methods, specifically UAVs and drones, pose the least risk. Further, when risk to human life can be reduced, and intelligence collection not impeded, it's no wonder commanders and decision makers seem to favor the technical collection methods over human collection methods. Casualties during war today are not near the numbers they were in previous conflicts and wars, and it is likely that anytime risk to or loss of human life can be averted, it will be.

When Hugh Jameson referred to UAVs and drones as the "platform of choice" for intelligence collection, it implies that UAVs and drones are certainly more relevant than other methods of collection, and that they are the go-to technical collection method for gathering intelligence, but can only gather what is available, or what is happening at a specific moment in time. UAV and drone pilots are not intelligence analysts, and do not have the cultural awareness and specific area knowledge to accurately decipher what the images see. Put simply, it's not their job. Likewise, when these video feeds or images are disseminated, with no analysis or cultural and area expertise applied, the viewer or end user will likely draw their own conclusions from the information collected. The technology is certainly not a bad capability to have, but the technology alone, with no human element present, is only giving half the picture. If a picture is truly worth one thousand words, then we should not settle for only five hundred. By adding the human factor, through a HUMINT team or intelligence analyst, we have the potential to add context and meaning that otherwise might have never been known, giving the commander or decision maker a more detailed picture.

The analysis points to an understanding that current technology can and should be exploited in collecting intelligence. The decrease in risk to human life, the immediate feedback or picture of what is happening on the ground, and the ability to see an operation unfold in real-time are clear advantages that technical collection capabilities provide a commander. Being able to operate from a distance, however, seems to be a double edged sword. While that advantage does provide less risk to human life, it also provides less fidelity and detail as to any predictive element or intentions of a threat, or any specific context for real time activities. With the reduction in drone strikes (Guy Taylor and Kristina Wong), senior leaders appear to understand that while UAVs and drones offer distinct advantages, they alone are not a sole answer for intelligence collection. With the addition of human collection and analysis, they can offer a more detailed, predictive product to the end user. While this may pose more risk, and take more time, it will ultimately give a better insight into the changing threat and environment that exists today.

Predictability through HUMINT Successes and Failures

Technical collection methods may be the favored capability, but can only give an indication of what is current, or what is happening at a specific moment in time; the present. UAVs and drones give accurate, detailed pictures of locations, movements, formations, and other relevant information pertaining to an enemy or threat, including lethal targeting of high-value individuals, but do not distinguish a threat actor from an ordinary civilian when dealing with a Hybrid Threat, or non-state actors. Further, the old saying that a picture is worth a thousand words may be true, but if the picture is unclear, blurry, or undecipherable, then one thousand words stating that are worthless. James Clapper cites the Hybrid and diverse threat as the worst he's seen in 50 years. However, this does not mean that we do not, or cannot understand it by incorporating current intelligence collection methods with technological advances. When we rely on technology alone, we lose the human insight and predictive aspect. How a person feels can affect how they act and make decisions, and technology, specifically UAVs and drones cannot provide this aspect. Mark Lowenthal states that because UAVs are operated remotely from miles away, they can get close to a target without being detected, or risking human life. However, when remotely operating a vehicle, from miles away, we completely eliminate the human element from our collection. All we can say is that this is what we see here and now. "Drones are a necessary tactic, but they are not a strategy."[51] UAVs and drones do not have the inherent capability of knowing a particular region or area, its people, their culture and their customs, and certainly UAV and drone operators are not trained in this area. Research suggests that UAVs and collection methods that are done from a safe distance do indeed lose the fidelity of having someone there who knows the people, situations, and has an understanding of the area or region. This does not mean though that these methods cannot provide value to a commander or decision maker. They

---

[51] Taylor, and Wong, "Drone Strikes Plummet as U.S. Seeks more Human Intelligence."

may, however, provide a more clear understanding by adding HUMINT capabilities in conjunction with UAVs, or having HUMINT analysts provide insight to the UAV's video feeds for increased situational awareness.

Reporting Issues: HUMINT is Underutilized, not Integrated or not Understood

When Lieutenant General William G. Boykin stated in his article that intelligence failures may be the result of analytically weak products, this is an area where human analysis needs to be applied and honed. Adding HUMINT collectors or trained HUMINT analysts can add fidelity to collected information that may give a more detailed insight into the intelligence already available, which may make products more useful to commanders and decision makers. Additionally, when reports are ignored entirely, then it does not matter how much is collected, but rather how much is used.

Clearly, when combat arms officers and maneuver commanders do not understand an intelligence collection capability, we as intelligence professionals have a problem, especially when this capability has been around for as long as conflicts have been fought. It is not their misunderstanding of the HUMINT discipline that makes it appear irrelevant, it is the intelligence professional's lack of explanation, compounded by complex reporting and over classification that make it appear irrelevant when compared to technology-based disciplines. The fascination with technological advances and the future of intelligence collection itself is not put ahead of any one collection discipline, but rather focuses on the fusion of all disciplines to produce a clearer picture. Further, by putting this clearer picture in the hands of the customers that need it most, is what makes it relevant. When intelligence reporting is either over classified, or extremely difficult to access or decipher, then it has become irrelevant, and not used, regardless of the collection discipline. When commanders do not use a HUMINT capability for intelligence collection, then an obvious lack of HUMINT reporting will be produced. When those same commanders see little to no useful intelligence reporting from their collection teams, they question the necessity of that specific capability, which often times leads to a complete dismissal of the asset. When Thomas Ricks, the author of *Fiasco: The American Military Adventure in Iraq, 2003 to 2005*, states that combat arms officers likely did not even understand the HUMINT capability, then how can actionable intelligence reporting even be expected to be seen as relevant to creating a clearer picture for commanders?

Reporting Issues: Intelligence Sharing and Incorporating Collection are where we fail

Some have made the argument that more is better, and you should not discount any intelligence reporting for fear of overlooking some detail that may prove important later. This is the area where we as intelligence professionals create roadblocks and obstacles for the dissemination of intelligence. From the beginning, we do no not do a good enough job of explaining how collection works, specifically, how each capability can enhance a commander's or decision maker's understanding of a threat or the environment. This is most likely not done intentionally, but rather through complacency. However, "At times, the information the S2 needs to arrive at a conclusion may be too difficult to obtain, so team databases or intelligence products may simply be stuffed with nuggets of information, in hopes that the user will find appropriately insightful items."[52]

---

[52] Boykin and Swanson, "'Operationalizing' Intelligence."

This is clearly not how intelligence reporting, sharing and dissemination were intended to help a commander. If an end-user has to find their own useful or insightful items, then we have clearly created our intelligence failure from the onset. The idea of intelligence is to provide the commander or decision maker with the most reliable, up to date information about a particular threat, region or event, and not to have them decipher from a set of clues or random pieces of information vaguely related to the topic. The way in which we share and disseminate intelligence will likely play a larger role with decreasing personnel and reduced budgets. The US Department of Justice recognizes this aspect, and has stated that "In developing our country's response to the threat of terrorism, public safety leaders from all disciplines have recognized the need to improve the sharing of information and intelligence across agency borders."[53]

After reviewing many reports, articles, and papers on the need for HUMINT, and whether or not a capability is still necessary, despite technological advancements, it appears that what is deemed more relevant or necessary is the fusion of the intelligence collection capabilities. Downsizing an organization such as the United States Army would necessitate a fused intelligence capability in order to capitalize on fewer resources and personnel. It is not necessarily about doing more with less, but rather doing better with what we have. Necessity will become apparent when personnel are reduced, and budgets shrink. Relevance will increase when collection capabilities fuse together.

Human Intelligence seemed to thrive as the premier intelligence collection discipline in early conflicts, and up until the early part of the 1900s it was the

---

[53] U.S. Department of Justice, *Fusion Center Guidelines*, "The Role of Leadership," accessed October 17, 2014, https://it.ojp.gov/default.aspx?area=nationalInitiatives&page=1181.

technologically advanced discipline. Where we see HUMINT successful, is when it is integrated with other disciplines in collecting and verifying information.

From the beginning of conflicts dating back to biblical times, HUMINT collection was seen as an absolute necessity to commanders, largely because that was the most advanced, and often times the only capability available to them. HUMINT produced reports that saw results in understanding the threat's actions and motivations. As technology advanced, it appears that we focused on the high-tech, and lost sight of the meaning or analysis of the intelligence produced. We lost sight of why we were collecting intelligence, and instead focused on how we were collecting it. Faster and immediate does not always mean better or more thorough. Ultimately, any specific intelligence collection discipline is irrelevant entirely if we are not answering the right questions for the commanders and decision makers. The reporting produced, and the analysis of that reporting is what commanders need to make decisions.

Human Intelligence can increase its relevancy as a collection discipline by integrating with other collection disciplines, including analysis. Having trained HUMINT collection teams integrated with analysts can help interpret technology-based collection information. By simply having a human element involved with the analysis of technology-based collection, we may be able to offer even more insight, or make that picture worth one thousand and two hundred words.

Furthermore, by making reporting more accessible to analysts, commanders, and decision makers, we can increase the chances of painting the clearest picture possible. Decision makers and commanders may not have time to sift through the multitude of intelligence reports available to them, but if we as intelligence professionals give them the ability to access intelligence reporting as easily as accessing a live UAV or drone feed, then we can at least put the information in the right hands. Overreliance on classifications to protect sources and methodology has made HUMINT reporting and techniques difficult to understand. Protection of clandestine sources is vital to ensuring that the flow of information can remain, but not at the expense of restricting the information itself.

Reductions in both HUMINT personnel and resources may be inevitable, but are not likely to affect HUMINT's role in future intelligence collection. A better merging of HUMINT and technology, both in collection and in analysis and dissemination, will produce a clearer picture for commanders and decision makers, offering near immediate feedback, detailed, insightful analysis, and decreased risk to human life.

<u>Improving Intelligence Sharing</u>

The concept of Intelligence Fusion Centers has been advanced by the US Department of Justice, as well as the US Department of Homeland Security. The US Department of Justices calls a Fusion Center: "an effective and efficient mechanism to exchange information and intelligence, maximize resources, streamline operations, and improve the ability to fight crime and terrorism by merging data from a variety of sources."[54]

The US military has similar centers, called Fusion Cells, used both in garrison and in theaters of operations, where multiple intelligence disciplines are collocated for the

---

[54] U.S. Department of Justice, *Fusion Center Guidelines*, Executive Summary Criminal Intelligence Sharing Plan, accessed October 17, 2014, https://it.ojp.gov/default.aspx?area=nationalInitiatives&page=1181.

44

purpose of intelligence analysis and sharing. The framework is in place for intelligence sharing, but it needs to be shared with more people than intelligence professionals.

Director of National Intelligence, James Clapper's view on fusion centers indicate that this is something intelligence professionals need to continue to foster for future threats and conflicts. "Fusion centers, which I think are a great step forward, something that didn't exist 10 years ago and there are now some 72 of them . . . there is a federal nexus to ensure that appropriately designated information is shared quickly with state and local officials."[55]

[55] James Clapper, *House and Senate Select Intelligence Committees' Joint Hearing on the Threats Against the United States Since September 11, 2001*, September 13, 2011, accessed October 19, 2014, https://it.ojp.gov/default.aspx?area=national Initiatives&page=1181.

CHAPTER 5

CONCLUSIONS AND RECOMMENDATIONS

Conclusions

Intelligence collection is essential in shaping the picture of a threat's intentions, both present and future, and therefore the only truly irrelevant intelligence is that which is not used. Hindsight can place blame on intelligence failures, but can also highlight where there was success.

HUMINT Reduction

Human Intelligence collection is not being reduced any more so than other collection methods and consequently will likely not suffer any great loss of capability. Intelligence leaders and decision makers recognize the changing threat and environment, and understand that intelligence collection must also change. Incorporating HUMINT collection, as well as human terrain analysts with technology based collection methods will only amplify and enhance the products produced. Whether we operate under the constraints of decreased budgets, personnel, or both, the collection of intelligence is vital to understanding the threat and environment. Through technology we have decreased the risk to human life, while increased our ability to gather more information. Leaders at all levels have stated the advantages of using UAVs in combat theaters, as well as for law enforcement, and have also stated that human analysis and interpretation is vital in adding detail and fidelity to that collected information.

HUMINT and Technology

Human Intelligence can enhance intelligence collection by combining with technology, rather than trying to keep up with it, or out pace it. But perhaps the greatest enhancement HUMINT can drive is the way in which intelligence and information is shared. Human analysis is the capability commanders and decision makers go to for answers in predicting future intentions. In today's hybrid, nationless threat environment, HUMINT can posture itself as more than just a collection discipline, but also a dissemination and sharing capability, that can bridge technology with human analysis.

HUMINT Reporting

Human Intelligence reporting is clunky, over-classified, and too attached to its clandestine roots. It is often blamed as a failure if it does not accurately predict or thwart attacks. As manpower is reduced and budget constraints are placed on the Intelligence Community, HUMINT collection must adapt to the changing environment, and will succeed and excel by better integrating and merging with advancing technological collection methods.

The basis for integrating multiple collection disciplines, along with analysis, is in place in the form of fusion centers, used in military and civilian organizations. Combat arms commanders need to be made aware of these fusions centers, and have easy access to reporting and products produced from them. The intelligence discipline plays a supporting role for the decision makers, and therefore needs to take the lead in explanation of how commanders and decision makers can access information.

Recommendations

Human Intelligence needs to be end-user friendly and incorporated into analysis easier. Access to intelligence reporting needs to be as easy as watching a video feed from a UAV, otherwise, it will never get read. When combat arms officers and commanders do not understand a capability, they are unlikely to use it. Intelligence professionals should be responsible in making reporting easily accessible to commanders and end-user customers. Intelligence collection is often times difficult, risky, and comes at a high cost. Similarly, intelligence professionals are responsible for explaining these risks and capabilities to commanders, and how these capabilities can benefit a commander's decision process. If combat arms officers are unfamiliar with a collection capability, then it is the intelligence officer's duty to explain the capability and its resources, and not the combat arms officers that need to figure it out.

Downsizing an organization, as well as financial constraints, is inevitable in today's military. We must keep pace with the Secretary of Defense and the President's directives. A smaller, more streamlined military is the future, but that does not mean that it is to be any less capable. Intelligence collection will always be a necessity, as the saying goes, "the enemy always has a vote," but how each collection discipline can increase its relevancy is by how they integrate together in order to paint the picture for the commander or decision maker.

Integration of multiple collection disciplines will produce more thorough, detailed intelligence products and reports. Tipping and cueing, where one intelligence collection discipline triggers the activation of another collection discipline to verify or enhance collection, must be the go-to methodology, rather than relying on one favored discipline.

Technology can be great, as can HUMINT . . . each provides unique aspects . . . we need to merge this, and create the mindset that we need "all" collection disciplines together. Stovepiping has to become a term of the past, where each collection discipline maintains separation from others, and especially from combat arms disciplines. Specialists in specific areas of intelligence collection are needed, but not at the expense of operating in isolation from other disciplines. Intelligence fusion, to include intelligence analysis, will produce the most detailed picture possible.

Intelligence Officers have to take the lead in how information is disseminated and shared. Intelligence Officers and professionals must be at the forefront of their profession in ensuring commanders know what each capability can add to the collection picture. It is not the job of the combat arms officer to figure out what intelligence does, or how it can help them . . . it is the other way around. We are failing as intelligence leaders when we do not champion collection methods and disciplines, and integrate methods together. Furthermore, if intelligence sharing and dissemination are deemed failures, we are responsible for correcting this.

Instead of asking the question of is this person or entity able to read these reports or products, we need to be asking is there any reason they cannot. Intelligence is bound by classification issues, which must be adhered to, as well as need to know guidelines, but it should not operate as an exclusionary organization first. As intelligence professionals, our default operating guidelines should be to find a way to share as much as we can, with as many as we can. Furthermore, we should always be looking for way ways to incorporate each discipline together, rather than focusing on how each collection discipline can operate within a specific environment. We need to find ways to mix collection methodologies, expand reporting, and incorporate our combat arms officers into the process.

Robert Steele states that technical intelligence collection will excel with HUMINT, and not alone. However, HUMINT can and must excel with technology as well, and cannot stand by trying to find ways to cling to old, outdated, clandestine heritage and not embracing and incorporating technological advances. If a picture is truly worth one thousand words, then we need to do all we can to ensure each and every word is relevant and read by as many commanders and decision makers as possible.

BIBLIOGRAPHY

Aldrich, Richard J., and John Kasuku. "Escaping from American Intelligence: Culture, Ethnocentrism and the Anglosphere." *International Affairs* 88, no. 5 (September 2012): 1009-1028.

Bay, Austin. "In the Absence of HUMINT." *The Washington Times*, July 31, 2003. Accessed May 13, 2014. http://www.washingtontimes.com/news/2003/jul/31/20030731-081957-6447r/?page=all.

Best Jr., Richard A. *Intelligence to Counter Terrorism: Issues for Congress*. Washington, DC: Congressional Research Service, May 2003.

Boykin, Lieutenant General William G., U.S. Army (ret.), and Scott Swanson, "'Operationalizing' Intelligence." *Special Warfare Bulletin* 6 (June 2008). Accessed September 22, 2014. http://www.army.mil/professionalWriting/volumes/volume6/june_2008/6_08_1_pf.html.

Brooks, Drew. "525th Military Intelligence Brigade unveiled on Fort Bragg." *Fayetteville Observer*. October 2014. Accessed October 17, 2014. http://www.fayobserver.com/news/local/th-military-intelligence-brigade-unveiled-on-fort-bragg/article_fa19cc96-f895-59f3-accb-eb9015281b15.html?mode=jqm.

Caruso, Robert. "Here's How the US Can Build the Intelligence Capabilities Needed to Defeat ISIS." *Business Insider*, September 2014. Accessed September 23, 2014. http://www.businessinsider.co.id/the-us-needs-better-humint-to-beat-isis-2014-9/#.VEWDybQo6P8.

Central Intelligence Agency. "The Capture and Execution of Colonel Penkovsky, 1963." Accessed September 23, 2014. https://www.cia.gov/news-information/featured-story-archive/2010-featured-story-archive/colonel-penkovsky.html.

Clapper, James. *House and Senate Select Intelligence Committees' Joint Hearing on the Threats Against the United States Since September 11, 2001*. September 13, 2011. Accessed October 19, 2014. https://it.ojp.gov/default.aspx?area=national Initiatives&page=1181.

Erwin, Marshall Curtis. *Intelligence, Surveillance, and Reconnaissance (ISR) Acquisition: Issues for Congress*. Washington, DC: Congressional Research Service, April 2013.

Headquarters, Department of the Army. Army Doctrinal Reference Publication 2-0, *Intelligence*. Washington, DC: Government Printing Office, August 2012.

———. Field Manual (FM) 2-22.3, *Human Intelligence Collector Operations*. Washington, DC: Government Printing Office, August 2006.

Hulnick, Arthur S. *Fixing the Spy Machine Preparing American Intelligence for the Twenty-First Century*. Westport, CT: Praeger, 1999.

Jameson, Hugh. "Drones between Satellite and Earth." *Armada International* 31, no. 6 (December 2007/January 2008): 40.

Joint Chiefs of Staff. Joint Publication (JP) 2-0, *Intelligence*. Washington, DC: The Joint Staff, 2013.

Kimmons, Lt. Gen. John F. "Intel Surge." *Aviation Week and Space Technology* 165, no. 19 (November 13, 2006).

Leary, Stephen. "Intelligence Budgets during the Clinton Years." September 2008. Accessed May 13, 2014. http://blog.stephenleary.com/2008/09/intelligence-budgets-during-clinton.html.

Lowenthal, Mark M. *Intelligence: From Secrets to Policy*. 5th ed., Washington, DC: CQ Press, 2012.

Margolis, Gabriel. "The Lack of HUMINT: A Recurring Intelligence Problem." *Global Security Studies* 4, no. 2 (Spring 2013): 43-60.

Ricks, Thomas E. *Fiasco: The American Military Adventure in Iraq, 2003 to 2005*. New York: The Penguin Press, 2006.

Roulo, Claudette. "Cuts Make Intelligence Failures Likely, Top Intel Official Says." *American Forces Press Service*, April 2013. Accessed May 15, 2014. http://www.defense.gov/news/newsarticle.aspx?id=119809.

Steele, Robert D. "Human Intelligence: All Humans, All Minds, All the Time." Monograph, Strategic Studies Institute, U.S. Army War College, May 2010.

Swan, Darin. "HUMINT Challenges in the Post 9/11 Era." August 2008. Accessed October 13, 2014. http://www.academia.edu/1460547/HUMINT_Challenges_in_the_Post-9_11_Era.

Taylor, Guy, and Kristina Wong. "Drone Strikes Plummet as U.S. Seeks more Human Intelligence." *The Washington Times*, October 9, 2013. Accessed September 23, 2014. http://www.washingtontimes.com/news/2013/oct/9/drone-strikes-drop-as-us-craves-more-human-intelli/?page=all.

Turner, Michael A. *Historical Dictionary of United States Intelligence*. Lanham, MD: Scarecrow Press, 2005.

U.S. Department of Justice. *Fusion Center Guidelines*. Accessed October 17, 2014. https://it.ojp.gov/default.aspx?area=nationalInitiatives&page=1181.

United States Senate Select Committee on Intelligence, *Report on the US Intelligence Community's Pre War Intelligence Assessments on Iraq*, July 2004.

Wilkinson, Colonel Kevin R., United States Army. "Unparalleled Need: Human Intelligence Collectors in the United States Army." Strategy Research Project, U.S. Army War College, Carlisle Barracks, PA, 2013.

Wobensmith, John C., and Jeff Smith. "Reinvigorating Intelligence." *The Journal of International Security Affairs* (Spring 2007). Accessed May 15, 2014. http://www.securityaffairs.org/issues/2007/12/wobensmith&smith.php.

www.ingramcontent.com/pod-product-compliance
Lightning Source LLC
Chambersburg PA
CBHW081120280526
45787CB00007B/2918